I0570741

7 KEYS TO UNLOCK YOUR POTENTIAL IN CHRIST

Steve & Laura Allmen

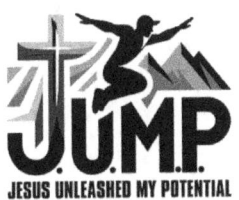

J.U.M.P.

JESUS UNLEASHED MY POTENTIAL

Copyright © 2024 | MATTHEW 25 29

PAPERBACK ISBN-13: 979-8-9902079-0-5

Version 1.1.2024 | March 2024

All rights reserved. No part of this publication may be reproduced, distributed, or transmitted in any form or by any means, including photocopying, recording, or other electronic or mechanical methods, without the prior written permission of the publisher, except in the case of brief quotations embodied in critical reviews and certain other non-commercial uses permitted by copyright law. For permission requests, write to the publisher at the address or email below.

Published by: MATTHEW 25 29

Steven Daniel Allmen

850 Meadowbrook Drive

Mount Pleasant, Michigan 48858

Content Editor: David Strauss

Cover Design: Barbara Wade

Contents

Introduction

Have you ever wondered what it truly means to unlock your fullest potential in Christ?

This question lies at the heart of our journey and the essence of why we wrote this book. We wanted to create a constant companion for your life's journey, a go-to guide for motivation, clarity, and fulfilling your life's purpose in Christ.

This is not intended as just a one-time read but a go-to resource for ongoing inspiration, clear guidance, and fulfillment of your life's mission. The insights that fill these pages have been transformative for us, guiding us to new heights of fulfillment as God consistently orchestrates our life's journey, opening and closing doors along the way.

The story of how this book came into existence is incredible, a continuation of a journey we began documenting in our first book, "Jesus Unleashed My Potential." The origins of both books can be traced back to 2015, when we made the choice to join a mission team from our church. We partnered with "Missions.me" for a short-term mission trip to the Dominican Republic. While there, in a modest, out-of-the-way town, we encountered a tangible sign of God's intentions for us—what we understand as prophecy.

Now, let's pause for a second to clarify what we mean by "prophecy." In our experience, a prophecy is a divinely inspired message handed down through a prophet—a person God has selected to be His messenger. A prophecy can be a warning, a statement, a detailed account, or even a glimpse into the future, all of which may be beyond our regular human comprehension.

During our mission trip, we met the local team that we'd be working with at their small church. As we all set out to walk to the area designated for our street ministry, Laura was introduced to an older woman—whom we guessed to be in her 70s—as the "Area Prophet." With the help of an interpreter, she began to speak to Laura about her future, describing a vision in which Laura was wielding a sword. At the time, Laura didn't grasp that this sword symbolized God's Word.

Once we had finished our morning of street ministry, we returned to the church for lunch. This is when the "Area Prophet" beckoned Laura over and started talking in more detail. She spoke about Laura and her family, revealing eerily accurate insights—things she couldn't have known otherwise. She then shifted her focus to Steve and his future, sharing detailed visions, including elements of our relationship and family life that she couldn't have known about. At this point, Steve, who was outside the church, was called in by an interpreter who had been listening in on the conversation. It was then prophesied that Steve would write a book, become an evangelist, and perform a life-altering prayer.

Following this spiritually intense episode—which was just our third day into our first-ever mission trip—neither of us felt entirely confident about the prophetic words spoken. Nevertheless, we chose to accept them as true and often found ourselves discussing them. Laura would jokingly warn Steve to avoid drinking bourbon, teasing that God wouldn't want an evangelist with whiskey breath.

Fast forward to the end of 2021. By this time, Steve had stepped away from his lifelong career in the automotive industry. The two of us found ourselves at a conference in Las Vegas, Nevada. During the first lunch break, attendees were free to pick from several restaurants for smaller group lunches. During lunch, we met David Strauss, an author and writing coach. David listened attentively to our story and offered his services to bring life to our book. Several weeks later, we reconnected to discuss our vision for the book, and David kindly offered to draft a preliminary introduction for our book. By 2022, the prophecy from years ago had materialized; we worked closely together for nearly six months and ultimately published "Jesus Unleashed My Potential."

Even though we never rolled out the red carpet for an official book launch or ventured down the well-trodden path of traditional marketing, our hearts were still searching, praying ceaselessly for clarity on what God truly wanted us to do with our book. Then, like a bolt of divine lightning, David Strauss reconnects with us in early 2023 for a virtual catch-up.

Would you believe it? He had a dream—a God-inspired vision—that cracked the code, answering the burning question that had been haunting us: Our first book was destined to ignite a movement, to serve as a stepping stone for unlocking others' divine potential! The second Laura heard David spill the words of his prophetic dream that we're meant to build a soul-stirring ministry around 'Jesus Unleashed My Potential,' she was electrified. A rush of exhilaration flooded her; she just knew, YES, this is our true calling.

United in this newfound purpose, the trio of us dove headfirst into strategizing the steps to lead others toward the life-altering realization that not only had 'Jesus Unleashed My Potential,' but He's ready to unleash yours too!

Jumping Into Your Full Potential

Jumping into your full potential in Christ doesn't mean you have to be perfect. It's really about recognizing you're the one steering your life, but you're using the wisdom from the Bible as your compass.

Imagine it as taking the wheel of your life's journey, with the Bible as your G.P.S., ready to guide you at every turn and decision. It's about making choices that reflect God's direction, not just going through the motions. This way, every day becomes an opportunity to align a little more closely with God's path for you, learning from each bump and curve along the road.

It isn't something that happens overnight or through grand, sweeping gestures. It's more like a tapestry woven from the threads of everyday decisions, actions, and the dreams we dare to chase—even when they seem out of reach.

Think about it this way: Each morning, we're faced with a choice. Do we hit the snooze button, or do we get up and spend a few quiet moments with God before the day rushes in? It's tempting to choose extra sleep, but those moments in prayer or with the Bible can set our course for the day. It's not about checking a box; it's about filling our tanks with the right fuel. And sure, there's no lightning bolt when we make that choice, but there's a subtle shift, a gentle nudging in the right direction.

Then there's the way we treat our bodies—our temples. It's easy to fall into habits that don't honor the incredible gift we've been given. I mean, who hasn't felt the pull of the couch over the call of the walking trail? But when we choose activities that make us stronger, food that nourishes instead of just filling, we're making a statement: we value what God has given us. It's not about vanity; it's about stewardship. And yes, sometimes that means choosing water over soda or a salad over fries—not always the easiest choice, but a meaningful one.

Our families see our faith in action more than anyone else. They're with us when we're deciding whether to hold onto a grudge or to extend forgiveness, engage in prayer, or let busyness take over. These choices, made in the crucible of everyday life, are our faith lived out loud. They're also our biggest opportunity to show what a life led by Christ looks like; messy, challenging, but ultimately, deeply rewarding.

And speaking of challenges, let's talk about having courage and battling self-judgment. Every dream planted in our hearts by God comes with its own set of giants. Sometimes, the biggest giant is our own inner critic, whispering that we're not smart enough, strong enough, or just plain not enough.

But here's where applied faith kicks in. It's choosing to step out anyway, to pursue that dream, to take that action—even when we're scared. Because faith isn't the absence of fear; it's moving forward in spite of it.

This applies to how we interact with our community, too. Being Christ's hands and feet might mean offering to help a neighbor, volunteering somewhere new, or simply showing kindness to a stranger. These actions might seem small, but they're powerful demonstrations of our faith. It's easy to underestimate the impact of a simple act of kindness, but in God's economy, nothing is wasted.

And when it comes to generosity, it's not just about what we give but how we give. Whether it's time, talent, or treasure, giving with a joyful heart is a reflection of our trust in God's provision. It's easy to cling tightly to what we have, especially in uncertain times. But generosity is an act of faith, a declaration that we believe God is our provider.

In essence, living your full potential in Christ is about making everyday choices that align with His will for our lives. It's about seeing the sacred in the ordinary, the divine opportunities in our daily routines. It's not always easy, and it's rarely straightforward. But it's a journey worth taking, one small step at a time.

In the everyday hustle, where faith meets pavement, that's where the magic happens. It's in the small choices, the quiet moments, and the simple acts of kindness that we find our rhythm with Jesus.

Now, as we lean into this journey a bit more, we're about to explore something special — the 7 Keys to J.U.M.P. with Jesus. This isn't about overhauling your life with impossible standards; it's about fine-tuning the way we live, breathe, and navigate our days with Him by our side.

Think of these keys as tools in your backpack, essentials for the adventure ahead.

- Unlock your mind
- Surrender your spirit
- Honor your body
- Bless your family
- Serve your community

- Give without measure

These are not just concepts; they're practical steps to unlocking a life where *"Jesus Unleashes My Potential."* So, let's take this leap together, unlock, surrender, honor, bless, serve, give, and stand in ways we never thought possible.

Unlocking
Your Mind

Romans 12:2 - "Do not conform to the pattern of this world but be transformed by the renewing of your mind."

The first key is all about unlocking our minds. Think about it: since the moment we were born, the outside world has been shaping us through our five senses. It's been crafting who we are, how we think, and how we make decisions. We've all developed a set of beliefs, or paradigms, that deeply affect us. At our core, we all want to belong, to fit in.

A perfect example of this is in a "Candid Camera" segment on conformity. Picture this: three employees face away from the elevator doors, and as people come in, they feel compelled to turn the same way. It's a simple yet powerful illustration of our desire to conform.

But here's the thing: the Bible is filled with instances where God asks us not to conform to the world's patterns. Take the Israelites in the wilderness, for instance. They kept wanting to go back to slavery, even when freedom was right there in front of them. They were stuck in their mindset. And aren't we sometimes like that? We hold onto mental chains that prevent us from growing and becoming who God created us to be.

These chains can be thoughts like "I am too old/young," "I am not smart enough," "I can't do it," or "No one will listen to me." It's incredible how we box ourselves in with these limiting beliefs. And the irony? Most of us don't even take the time to listen to what we're telling ourselves. Our biggest obstacles often lie within our own minds.

Philippians 4:8 encourages us to focus on things that are true, honorable, just, pure, lovely, and commendable. It's about setting our minds on higher, noble things and opening up new possibilities. The question is, are we willing to do the work to unlock our minds?

Practicing this means delving into scriptures, meditating on the teachings of Jesus, and praying for discernment. We've learned the importance of guarding our hearts and minds because they shape our words and actions. Memorizing and meditating on God's Word offers us protection, allowing our minds to be continually transformed. Verses like Proverbs 4:23, Psalm 119:11, and Colossians 3:16 are not just words; they are lifelines.

Over the years, we've been blessed with mentors who've held us accountable and taught us tools to renew our minds and change our paradigms. This isn't a quick fix; it's a journey. Depending on what we're working on, it can take as little as 3 weeks or several months. A mentor's guidance is crucial, especially in the beginning, as trying something different can be a real challenge.

One of the tools we've embraced is goal setting. We've created vision boards to help us visualize achieving our goals. If you're not familiar, a vision board is like a scrapbook of pictures of dreams and goals you want to accomplish. For example, it could be a cut out from magazines or newspapers. When we look at our boards, we don't just see images; we connect with them emotionally, believing in their possibility. This practice has helped us to see beyond our current circumstances.

We also write down our goals on laminated cards and place them where we'll see them often. Every time we touch a goal card, it triggers the feeling and vision associated with it. Each morning, we write down our goals with gratitude, using positive action language. It's about reinforcing to our subconscious mind that we've already achieved our goals. This practice helps us stay focused and minimizes distractions.

Speaking our goals is another key tool. Verses like Proverbs 18:21 and Matthew 12:36-37 remind us of the power of our words. So, we start each day by speaking our goals and scriptures aloud, setting a foundation of achievement and faith.

Is it really that simple? In essence, yes. But simple doesn't always mean easy. The story of the Israelites teaches us that. They had to rely on God, day by day, trusting in His provision, even when it was hard to let go of their old ways.

Laura's personal story is a powerful example of this. Faced with a difficult pregnancy and subsequent health challenges, she turned to these principles we've been talking about. Using mindset tools coupled with prayer, she experienced a remarkable healing. It's a testament to the power of renewing our minds.

Unlocking our minds is a daily practice. It involves visualization, attaching emotion to our visions, writing them down, and speaking them into existence.

APPLIED FAITH

Alright, diving into unlocking your mind, here are three steps to start shifting how you think and see the world:

1. **Make Friends with a Journal:** Every day, take a little time to write down some thoughts. Not just any thoughts. Focus on the good stuff—what you're grateful for, something good that happened, or a nice thing someone said. This helps shift your focus from the not-so-great to the awesome things around you.

2. **Focus on the Good Stuff:** Each morning, while you're brushing your teeth or having your coffee, think of one positive thing you're looking forward to in the day. Could be anything – a chat with a friend, your favorite lunch, or just the drive home listening to tunes. It's about tuning your antenna to the good vibes.

3. **Talk It Out Loud:** End your day by saying out loud three things you're thankful for. It doesn't matter if your only audience is your cat or a houseplant. Speaking gratitude into the air makes it more real and helps shift your mindset from "I lack" to "I have."

These aren't magic spells, but more like habits. The more you do them, the more you start to notice the chains in your mind loosening up, making space for new thoughts and possibilities.

DEVOTIONAL DECREE

I decree that I am renewing my mind daily as I meditate on God's word. Romans12:2 states "Do not be conformed to this world but be transformed by the renewal of your mind." I fix my eyes on Jesus, and I choose to believe His word. I take every thought that comes into my mind captive. I bind and cast out all negative and defeating thoughts in the name of Jesus.

I fix my eyes on the truth that I am fearfully and wonderfully made Psalm 139:14. created in Gods image with a plan and a purpose for my life. I decree and declare that "No weapon formed against me will prosper" Iasiah54:17 I am happy, I am able, and I am capable. The Lord is with me wherever I go. He is my light and my salvation. I open my mind to the fullness of God and embrace the limitless potential through faith and the power of God's word.

Surrender Your Spirit

"Trust in the Lord with all your heart and lean not on your own understanding; in all your ways submit to him, and he will make your paths straight."
Proverbs 3:5-6:

Purpose: Give yourself fully to the Lord, trusting in His plans for your life.

What does it mean to give yourself fully to the Lord, trusting in His plans for your life? It has taken us many years to truly understand and act to the level required to do this. Doing this is a transformation, an act of faith, and a deep commitment. As humans, we are formed through our experiences.

What we have seen, heard, and participated in. Our outside world has helped us form who we are. Aligning our lives, decisions, and wants with God's will and purpose shows that, through our thoughts and actions, we recognize God as the ultimate source of guidance, wisdom, and love in our lives.

Jeremiah 1:5 (ESV): "Before I formed you in the womb I knew you, and before you were born, I consecrated you; I appointed you a prophet to the nations."

In the Bible, God speaks to Jeremiah, revealing to him that God had a plan and purpose for him even before he was conceived. God appointed Jeremiah to be a prophet to the nations, beginning his ministry and revealing to him that God knew him intimately even before he was born. We believe God has a plan and purpose for each one of us, and He has placed that in our hearts. Through our own free will, each of us can choose whether it is fulfilled.

Trusting in God and His plans for us is really a lifelong journey. It is a journey of believing, a journey of faith. It is one thing to believe; it is another to have faith. We can believe, based on facts, things that we have seen or experienced. The strength of our belief can fluctuate depending on the information or experience each of us has. Faith takes us beyond belief. It involves a level of trust, a level of conviction, and a level of confidence without having logical proof that something is possible or will happen.

Faith is absolute assurance and confidence that the outcome is in God's hands. Sometimes, we must surrender our own desires that exist in our flesh to pursue those that God has placed in our hearts. Trusting in God involves an unwavering belief that He does have a plan and purpose for each of us and that everything that comes upon us can be used as a Blessing to be incorporated into His design for us. By seeking His guidance through studying His word, prayer, meditation, and listening to the Holy Spirit, even in the most difficult or most promising of times, we will maintain the path He desires for us.

Romans 8:28 (ESV) "And we know that in all things God works for the good of those who love him, who have been called according to his purpose."

Practice: Daily surrender through prayer, expressing your dependence on Jesus, and asking for His guidance in every step.

For us, learning to surrender our Spirit to God truly has been a lifelong journey. Sometimes, we find our flesh convincing us we have surrendered to God; however, when reflecting and seeking His explanations, sometimes we are deceived.

For example, there was a time that I was asked, along with my ministry co-leader, to coordinate moving a couch that was offered to a family who had just relocated from Europe to work in the US. Out of obligation, we both agreed to do so. After a few weeks, the person asked again if the couch was going to be moved; neither of us had done anything. So, out of knowing the right thing to do was to move the couch, I recruited Laura to assist.

After service, I rented a trailer, went to the person's house, picked up the couch, which was a project to get out the front door, and delivered it to the people who were expecting it.

When I arrived, I honestly felt a little guilty as they had no couch in their living room. I was bringing it for them. And it had been several weeks. In any case, the good deed was done, and I returned the rental equipment and thought nothing more of it.

Later that evening, I noticed a red dot on my hand between my thumb and index finger. Really didn't think much of it; I tried to wash it off but with no success. The next day, my hand was swollen and had dark circles around the red dot. Turns out, I had been bitten by a brown recluse spider. A concerning discovery. Coupled with fervent prayer for healing, Laura found some great natural treatment for the bite, and thankfully, I fully recovered in a couple of weeks. However, frankly, I was mad at God and had a conversation with Him. After all, I was doing His work; I was doing a good deed, making a difference for someone else in His Kingdom. Why did this spider bite me? To answer me, He gave me a dream. In the dream, when I went to do something good, and I had not asked God whether it was His will that I do it, I was placed in a dark pod on some type of ride.

The ride was not good, scary, and painful. Alternatively, when I wanted to do something good, and I asked God first whether it was His will that I do it, I was placed in a light pod on this ride. The ride was smooth, enjoyable, and extremely fun.

The takeaway is to surrender my Spirit to God and ensure that the actions I am taking are in alignment with His purpose.

In the example, the task may have been meant for my ministry co-leader to take and learn from. By taking action to get the job done, I may have taken away his opportunity. Through the dream, God had shown me the difference.

"I have been crucified with Christ. It is no longer I who live, but Christ who lives in me. And the life I now live in the flesh I live by faith in the Son of God, who loved me and gave himself for me."
Galatians 2:20 (ESV)

So, how can we work towards daily surrender? We work to apply several practical things to help us.

Daily Devotions: We start each day with time dedicated to reading the Bible and praying to God. Giving thanks, seeking His guidance, and sharing our concerns with Him. This provides a moment of surrender, placing our trust in God's plan for us for the day ahead. Similarly, we end each day the same way, in prayer, offering gratitude and prayer for others. We find ending our day this way allows us to focus on the positive results that have been provided to us. Always know there is good in all things that happen; we just must find it.

"Do not be anxious about anything, but in everything by prayer and supplication with thanksgiving let your requests be made known to God. And the peace of God, which surpasses all understanding, will guard your hearts and minds in Christ Jesus." Philippians 4:6-7 (ESV)

Journaling: We have found that doing this daily drives us to reflect on our thoughts, emotions, and events that have occurred.

We focus on gratitude when we journal.

In doing so, we are opening our minds and surrendering our innermost thoughts, inviting His wisdom and guidance into our spirit. Looking back at previous writing, it provides documented evidence of our spiritual growth over time.

"Rejoice always, pray without ceasing, give thanks in all circumstances; for this is the will of God in Christ Jesus for you." 1 Thessalonians 5:16-18

Acts of Kindness and Service. We have found such joy in living in alignment with our faith and values. Over and over, we surrender our desires, which are typically wrapped around personal gain, in exchange for serving others. Whether it is doing something for our children and grandchildren, volunteering, or simply being pleasant and welcoming to anyone we run into on a given day, by taking action around serving others, our ego becomes surrendered to God.

"Do nothing from selfish ambition or conceit, but in humility count others more significant than yourselves. Let each of you look not only to his own interests but also to the interests of others." Philippians 2:3-4 (ESV)

Potential: When you yield your spirit, you move in harmony with divine will, resulting in peace, joy, and spiritual growth.

So often, people find themselves in the midst of a storm, focusing on the storm, giving it strength, driving our thoughts, feelings, and ultimately our actions, ensuring it continues to grow. When we focus on what we see, hear, smell, taste, and feel, typically, that is what we will receive. If we focus on Him, regardless of physical circumstance, trust Him, and be obedient, we will find peace.

"You keep him in perfect peace whose mind stays with you because he trusts in you." Isaiah 26:3 (ESV)

Here is an example that Laura and I have gone through in the recent past. Our main sources of income are tied to investments that provide passive income. We have businesses that produce income but are still growing to a point where they can sustain our current standard of living on a regular basis. In late 2021, one of the investments began to have issues with providing regular inbound payments. We began to be concerned, focusing on the potential negative impacts. Our conversations were adversarial in nature, and we were not supportive or uplifting around the organization that was obligated to provide the payments. We enrolled others in our tale of woes, further exacerbating our feelings and conversations. Without realizing it, we were giving this storm life.

Soon, over the next 12-15 months, the same thing began to happen with other investments; our actions were the same, building on the negative, filling ourselves with doubt and worry. Ultimately, more than 10 different investments were not providing payments as expected. Not just for a month, this was all of them, for well over 6 months. We had created quite the hurricane, a category 5, if you were to measure it. Virtually no income. During this time, yes, we prayed to God, asking Him to intervene, asking Him what the lesson was in this, what we did or did not do that was causing this. Our prayers were focused on what was happening in the storm, focused on the effects of the storm, and focused on the worldly impacts.

There came a point where God provided a subtle answer to us both. We moved our rutter just a small amount back in 2021. Our focus shifted just the tiniest bit from His will for us to how we were to amass a large amount of money to be able to affect what we were doing to help others in God's Kingdom.

"Therefore, do not be anxious, saying, 'What shall we eat?' or 'What shall we drink?' or 'What shall we wear?' For the Gentiles seek after all these things, and your heavenly Father knows that you need them all. But seek first the kingdom of God and his righteousness, and all these things will be added to you." Matthew 6:31-33 (ESV)

By releasing all the issues we were holding to God and realigning ourselves with His word, He has delivered to us our every need, and at no time during this period were we in a position to not be able to make a payment, buy a meal, or provide help to others.

He provided a way. Our God is great.

Fully surrendering your spirit is a daily journey. Only through prayer, reflection, and communication with God can we keep our focus on Him. Seeking Him first.

Where are you today?

What possibilities are there that you are potentially stifling due to your focus shifting to the world? Incorporate these tools and begin to create a relationship with Him that will help you find a level of peace beyond understanding.

APPLIED FAITH

1. **Pause for a moment with God.** In the morning, take a brief pause to acknowledge His presence—like a quiet nod to the one who's got your day in hand. At night, a simple "thank you" for the day can be a powerful bookend.

2. **Spotlight the good.** Each day, find one thing that felt right or good, and acknowledge it. It's about training your eye to see the light, even on cloudy days.

3. **Act with kindness.** A kind word, a small favor, a moment of your time—these are tiny echoes of God's love through you. Look for a chance to make someone's day a bit brighter.

These steps are about weaving meaningful, faith-driven actions into the fabric of your everyday life, gently aligning your days with the grace and guidance of God.

DEVOTIONAL DECREE

Thank you, God, for a new day and your mercies that are new. Today, I come before you and surrender all my worries, fears, doubts, and anxieties. I lay all my stress at your feet. I trust in your word and your promises. I claim Proverbs 3:5- 6: "Trust in the Lord with all your heart, lean not on your own understanding.

In all your ways acknowledge Him, and He will make your paths straight." I decree that I walk in victory because the Lord is my strength. I release and let go. I release and let go; I release and let go.

I trust in my heavenly father and lay my life and my plans at your feet. God, you are good, and your mercies endure forever. Thank you, Father, for putting my trust in you right now. I am All that God created me to be. I am a child of the most high God.

Honor Your Body

"Do you not know that your bodies are temples of the Holy Spirit, who is in you, whom you have received from God? You are not your own; you were bought at a price. Therefore, honor God with your bodies."
1 Corinthians 6:19-20

The above scripture isn't just a reminder; it's a directive to recognize our bodies as temples of the Holy Spirit and to treat them with the respect they deserve.

Consider this: our bodies, crafted and provided by God, are truly miraculous. When we think about honoring our bodies, it's easy to focus only on the physical aspect. But our bodies are more than that. They're equipped with an immune system, an inflammatory response for tissue repair, and even the capability to repair DNA. Our cells regenerate approximately every four months, and our hormones regulate body functions. Proper nutrition provides the building blocks for cell repair and regeneration. Moreover, our nervous system, along with our mental and emotional well-being, significantly impacts our bodily functions.

Genesis 1:27 reminds us, "So God created man in his own image, in the image of God he created him; male and female he created them." Our bodies are more than physical entities; they're representations of God's image, temples where the Holy Spirit resides. Caring for our bodies means caring for both our physical and spiritual well-being.

In today's fast-paced world, it's all too easy to adopt a lifestyle that deteriorates our physical, mental, and spiritual health. Our diets often consist of processed foods, sugars, saturated fats, and artificial additives, leading to chronic health conditions and obesity. Many of us lead sedentary lives, spending much of our day in front of screens. Additionally, the constant pursuit of material success often overshadows our spiritual health, leading to increased anxiety or depression.

Matthew 11:28 offers solace, saying, "Come to me, all who labor and are heavily laden, and I will give you rest." Psalm 104:14-15 also reflects on the goodness of God's provision: "You cause the grass to grow for the livestock and plants for man to cultivate, that he may bring forth food from the earth and wine to gladden the heart of man, oil to make his face shine and bread to strengthen man's heart."

Using ourselves as an example, we've experienced the struggles of maintaining mental and physical health while living a typical American lifestyle. With the birth of our first son, our lives became a whirlwind of work and responsibilities. Steve juggled two jobs and part-time college while Laura worked evenings and weekends. Our hectic pace led us to rely on fast food and neglect exercise.

It took us ten years to take our first vacation without our children. We were so caught up in chasing the American dream that it led to significant health issues. Steve developed Crohn's disease, high blood pressure, pre-diabetes, and even contracted meningitis. From our tenth to about our twenty-fifth anniversary, we made several attempts to take control of our health. We explored various diets and exercise regimens and joined a vitamin company to educate ourselves and others about bodily health.

However, it wasn't until a loud message from God that we began to make earnest changes.

Job 8:7 promises, "And though your beginning was small, your latter days will be very great." Revelation 2:19 echoes this, saying, "I know your works, your love and faith and service, and patient endurance, and that your latter works exceed the first."

Practicing good health means balanced nutrition, regular exercise, and proper rest while avoiding harmful habits and substances.

There isn't a magic pill for health. Over the years, we've learned a lot about mental, physical, and spiritual health. We've transformed ourselves physically, losing weight, gaining muscle, and improving our cardiovascular health, and we take blood tests to measure and track our progress. Achieving results comes through consistent improvement, not a singular destination of perfection.

Balanced Nutrition: Proper nutrition is crucial. Drinking plenty of water each day is essential for bodily functions. We start each day with a 16-ounce glass of water, refreshing our cells. We've also minimized our intake of processed foods, sugars, and additives, using an app to help limit these in our diet. We've cut down on fast food, pork, and dairy and have incorporated Juice Plus into our regimen, bridging the gap between what we eat and what we should eat.

Regular Exercise: Being active is important, but it's about the right kind of exercise. We've learned the importance of proper technique, time, and intensity in our workouts. Working with a coach or trainer has provided us with amazing results. Exercising together at the gym 4-6 days a week not only improves our health but also strengthens our relationship.

Proper Rest: Quality sleep is vital for physical recovery, immune function, and mental clarity. We've learned to hydrate well while limiting liquids before bed and cutting off caffeine and alcohol several hours before sleep. Establishing a consistent sleep schedule and creating a bedtime routine that includes relaxing activities like reading, taking a bath, or prayer and meditation has improved the quality of our sleep.

Psalm 127:2 offers wisdom, "It is in vain that you rise up early and go late to rest, eating the bread of anxious toil; for he gives to his beloved sleep."

Potential: When we align our physical care with our spiritual care, we become more energetic, healthier, and ready to serve God's purpose.

By improving our nutrition, exercise, and rest, we're not just caring for our bodies; we're enhancing our potential to live a fulfilling life and reducing health risks. These areas are cornerstones of a healthy lifestyle, offering an exponential return on investment if we're willing to make changes and develop the discipline to turn our actions into habits.

For us, the transformation has been incredible, resulting in less time and money spent on medical treatment, a revitalized body and mind, and a deeper enjoyment of learning about our bodies each day. Imagine what a 1% improvement each day could mean for you in the long term. The information is available; it's up to you to decide and take action. Using the keys outlined in this book, you can unlock your potential.

APPLIED FAITH

Reflecting on the journey towards better health and spiritual well-being, here are three straightforward steps you can take to start aligning your physical care with your faith:

1. **Make one healthier food choice each day.** Start simple. Swap out a snack for a piece of fruit or choose water over soda. It's the small changes that gradually lead to big results.

2. **Move a little more.** Instead of aiming for a marathon, add a little extra movement to your day. Take a short walk, stretch in the morning, or do a few minutes of exercise. Find joy in being active in a way that feels good to you.

3. **Find rest and reflection time.** Dedicate a few minutes before bed to unwind and talk to God, maybe through prayer or meditation. This isn't just about getting better sleep; it's about nurturing your spirit along with your body.

These steps aren't about overnight transformation but about starting a journey where every small choice adds up to a healthier, more fulfilled you, both physically and spiritually.

DEVOTIONAL DECREE

Lord, you are good! As I go about my day today, I declare and decree that my body is a temple of the Holy Spirit. I choose to honor my body by taking good care of it. I will eat nourishing foods to help sustain all my organs and tissues. I declare today that my body functions properly and pain-free as it was created by God to function. I declare healing to every cell in my body. I say sickness and disease have no place in me, and in the name of Jesus, I bind all infirmities from my body.

Lord, your word says in Isaiah 53:5, "But He was wounded for our transgressions. He was bruised for our iniquities; the chastisement for our peace was upon Him, and by His stripes I am healed." I am healthy, I am healed, and I am restored in mind, body, and spirit. Thank you, God, for your word and your promises. Thank you for being my healer.

Bless Your Family

"Bear with each other and forgive one another if any of you has a grievance against someone. Forgive as the Lord forgave you."
Colossians 3:13

I n today's world, with all its challenges and divisions, it's super easy to get caught up in endless arguments and stress. But, taking a leaf from the Bible, we find some pretty solid advice on looking after the people in our lives. It's got these gems that help us feel less alone and more appreciated, even when things get tough. It reminds us that family isn't just the folks who share our DNA. It's about the people we choose to have close to us—our grandparents, aunts, uncles, mothers, fathers, brothers, sisters, the friends who've become like family, and everyone else who holds a special place in our hearts. It's about creating a circle of care and support, not defined by bloodlines but by love and mutual respect.

Ephesians 5:25 teaches us, "Husbands love your wives, as Christ loved the church and gave himself up for her." And in Matthew 22:36-40, we're reminded of the greatest commandments: to love God with all our heart, soul, and mind, and to love our neighbor as ourselves. These commandments lay the groundwork for building and maintaining strong family relationships.

We've learned the importance of reflection. By pausing to consider the other person's perspective, we can transform potentially volatile situations. It's about understanding what drives others' reactions. Our words are incredibly powerful, as Proverbs 15:1 tells us: "A soft answer turns away wrath, but a harsh word stirs up anger."

What would it look like to love those in our family circle with the same passion Christ had for the church? Proverbs 22:6 advises us, "Train up a child in the way he should go; even when he is old, he will not depart from it." This verse speaks volumes about the lasting impact of our guidance and example on our children, friends, and associates.

Practice: The way forward involves spending quality time with family members, offering support, cultivating forgiveness, and ensuring open communication.

Through studying the Bible and learning from hands-on experience, we've gained a deeper understanding of the importance of family. We've grown in our capacity to be more accepting and understanding, replacing excuses with efforts to show up for others. We are relational beings. Without strong relationships, our personal growth is hindered, and we lack a sense of fulfillment and connection. Recognizing that relationships provide emotional security, reduce stress, and offer opportunities for personal development and shared experiences has been transformative for us.

One of the changes we've implemented is to ensure we're face-to-face with people as often as possible. Whether it's with our immediate family, a mastermind group, a Bible study group, or a church ministry team, spending time in communication fosters belonging, satisfaction, and a sense of purpose. When feeling frustrated or slighted, we now look to understand the other's perspective, focusing on love and forgiveness. This approach may not always be easy, but it consistently places us in a position of peace and enables us to provide support and encouragement.

We go the extra mile, literally, to connect with people, believing that time spent with others is invaluable. We use our travel time to call family members, read, or listen to books, podcasts, or messages, further renewing our minds and expanding our ability to serve others.

Ephesians 4:32 encourages us to be kind and tenderhearted, forgiving one another as Christ forgave us. This principle has become central to how we interact with our family.

Potential: When we root our families in Christ's love, they become pillars of support, encouragement, and growth for each member.

We've crafted a vision for our family, placing God at the forefront of all we do. Through this lens, we work towards the dream we envision for our family life. Living this dream is a blessing. We engage in meaningful discussions about worldly culture and family values, strengthening our bond and resolve. Our adherence to Biblical principles has made us and our family stronger. We've observed the influence of various circles on our children, especially during their college years. Thankfully, the seeds of knowledge, wisdom, and goodness we planted in them have helped guide them through these influences. As they grow older, we see them returning to the fundamental values we taught them through God's word. It's heartening to see them passing these values to their children.

Proverbs 27:17, "Iron sharpens iron, and one man sharpens another," rings true for us. Are you living your dream life? Are the people you surround yourself with lifting you up and helping you grow? Are you serving others in the same way? Fostering relationships filled with forgiveness, love, respect, and nurturing brings immense fulfillment. We hope our journey inspires you to strengthen your family bonds and create a legacy of love and respect.

APPLIED FAITH

Given the heartfelt message about family, love, and the wisdom found in scripture, here are three straightforward actions to bring these insights into your daily life:

1. **Make Time for Heart-to-Hearts:** Carve out moments in your day or week dedicated solely to catching up with family members or close friends. This could be a coffee chat, a walk in the park, or a quiet sit-down at home. The key is giving undivided attention, showing you value them and their place in your life.

2. **Practice the Pause:** Before reacting in any heated or potentially stressful situation, take a deep breath and consider the other person's viewpoint. This moment of pause can help diffuse tension and lead to more understanding interactions. Remember, it's not about who's right but how you can solve things together.

3. **Commit to Acts of Kindness:** Small gestures of kindness can strengthen bonds tremendously. Whether it's doing a chore someone else dislikes, sending an encouraging note, or simply offering a listening ear, these acts of service speak volumes. Aim to do at least one kind thing for a family member or friend each day, reflecting the love and forgiveness taught in Ephesians 4:32.

By incorporating these actions into your routine, you not only enrich your personal relationships but also create a nurturing environment where everyone feels valued and supported.

DEVOTIONAL DECREE

This is the day that the Lord has made, and I will rejoice and be glad in it (Psalm 188:24). I declare that today my family is united. I decree peace in all conversations. My family is a blessing from the Lord. I choose to see my family as God sees it - happy, healthy, and whole. Right now, I speak the name of Jesus over my family. I speak of love, compassion, understanding, forgiveness, and prosperity over my family. In the name of Jesus, I cast out every lying spirit that would try to divide or deceive us.

We can do all things through Christ, who strengthens us. (Phil 4:13) We hold fast to your word and your commands, and we choose to love each other daily, forgiving offenses and moving forward in God's plan. Thank you, God, for families. Your word says in Psalm 68:6, "God sets the solitary in families; He brings out those who are bound into prosperity; but the rebellious dwell in a dry land." Thank you, God, for bringing me into your family.

Serve Your Community

*Galatians 5:13: "For you were called to freedom, brothers.
Only do not use your freedom as an opportunity for the flesh,
but through love serve one another."*

This scripture isn't just something to read; it's a call to live out, to truly embody the servant heart of Jesus by reaching out and touching the lives around us.

You know, in today's world, it seems like personal gain and material success often overshadow the importance of serving our community. With social media and digital communication, we're drifting into more isolation and fewer meaningful face-to-face relationships. This shift is impacting our ability to build bonds and enhance the local communities we're part of.

Philippians 2:3-4 gives us a powerful reminder: "Do nothing from selfish ambition or conceit, but in humility count others more significant than yourselves." For Laura and me, the hustle of life, culture, and the drive to get ahead financially did slow down our involvement in community service. But we never let it slip away entirely. Serving others has been a path of personal growth and humility for us. It keeps us grounded, reminding us that it's people, not possessions, that truly make a difference. Whether it was the local Parent Teacher Organization, Church Outreaches, the Humane Society, or the Homeowners Association, getting involved has often led us to lead by example. And you know, it's inspiring to see how our actions encourage others, including our kids, to serve as well. The more we chose to serve, the more we found ourselves looking for and participating in opportunities, driving us to a greater passion for loving and serving others. Our mission? To leave anyone God places in our path better off than before they met us.

1 Corinthians 12:25 really hits home: "That there may be no division in the body, but that the members may have the same care for one another." Serving isn't just about the actions we take; it's about the spiritual growth and the deeper connections it fosters. It's amazing how serving others can enrich not only our relationship with God but also bring us closer to people we might never have connected with otherwise.

Practice: So, what does it look like to serve your community? It's about volunteering, helping out your neighbors, getting involved in church activities, and looking for ways to make a positive impact.

I used to wonder, "I'm just one person; what difference can I make?" But let me tell you, the more we stepped out and said yes, the more comfortable we became with serving. Taking that first step might seem daunting, but the joy and fulfillment you find on the other side... it's something else. You find yourself wanting to jump again and again.

Our journey in serving together really took shape during our second year of marriage when we were living in Korea. We volunteered through our local church to deliver supplies to an orphanage. It wasn't much work, but the feeling of making a real impact, of connecting with those kids, left us with a deep sense of accomplishment. And it's moments like these that make you truly grateful for the hearts of those who run such places, often at great personal cost.

For Laura, getting involved in our kids' school PTO was an eye-opener. She learned so much – from fundraising to effective communication, budgeting, and running public forums. Every time she got involved, she not only developed new skills but also formed new friendships. It was more than just giving back; it was about personal growth, too.

One of the most impactful experiences for us as a family was joining a short-term mission trip to the Dominican Republic. The entire family was on a mission team – something new for all of us. The training, the relationships we built, and the experiences we had there... each day was an adventure that allowed us to make a significant impact and left us overflowing with gratitude. That trip changed our family in ways we couldn't have imagined, deepening our commitment to serving our community and beyond.

Potential: When you choose to serve, the growth and fulfillment you experience are immeasurable.

The beauty of serving is that each one of us has something unique to offer. 1 Peter 4:10 tells us, "As each has received a gift, use it to serve one another as good stewards of God's varied grace." Choosing to serve brings a profound sense of purpose and fulfillment. You see the positive impact of your actions on the lives of others, which brings immense joy. Serving cultivates compassion and empathy, connecting us with people from all walks of life. It's a way to step away from our own stress, focusing instead on the needs of others. Serving creates a win-win situation, enriching everyone involved and spreading positivity and well-being.

So, what would it look like if you decided to leap into serving your community? Whether it's your first time or you're returning to it, imagine the joy, the growth, and the difference you can make. Serving isn't just about what you give; it's also about what you gain – a richer, more compassionate life. Let's jump in and make that difference together.

APPLIED FAITH

Reflecting on the essence of serving and the personal growth it brings, here are three steps to start making a difference in your community:

1. **Look Around You:** Start by noticing the needs in your immediate community. A neighbor could use some help with yard work, or a local food bank is looking for volunteers. It's often the small acts of kindness that pave the way for bigger impacts.

2. **Say Yes More:** Next time an opportunity to help out or volunteer comes up, go for it. It might be helping organize an event at your kids' school or joining a cleanup day in your neighborhood. Don't underestimate the power of showing up and giving your time.

3. **Share Your Skills:** Think about what you're good at and enjoy doing, then find a way to share that with others. If you're handy, offer to fix things for those who can't. Love to cook? Prepare a meal for a friend who's going through a tough time. Everyone has something valuable to offer.

DEVOTIONAL DECREE

Today is a great day. I am blessed to be part of the community I am placed in. I declare that my community is my responsibility. I declare that as for me and my house, we will serve the Lord (Joshua 24:15). Today, for everyone that comes into my path, I will be a light for them. I will do my best to love all those around me, especially those that don't agree with me. I choose to serve others, and by doing so, I am being a light in the darkness.

God, your world matters to you, so it matters to me. I am stepping into the lives of those around me and making a positive impact. I can serve others with a smile, give without a measure of my time, talents, and finances, and be a difference maker and a hope dealer. Lord, may your Holy Spirit live through me as I go about my day. I will not become weary in doing, for you are with me. God bless my community with peace and prosperity. In Jesus' name. Amen

Give Without Measure

"Give, and it will be given to you. A good measure, pressed down, shaken together, and running over, will be poured into your lap. For with the measure you use, it will be measured to you." —Luke 6:38

The wisdom in the Bible about giving is profound. It teaches us about the joy and purpose behind giving freely, without any anticipation of receiving something in return. Whether it's our time, talents, or treasures, giving from the heart is what truly pleases God. Over the years, Laura and I have delved into many messages about giving. We've come across views that paint it as an obligation but also teachings that emphasize giving as an act of love, something that should naturally spring from our hearts, bringing joy and fulfillment.

Mark 4:8 speaks to this, "And other seeds fell into good soil and produced grain, growing up and increasing and yielding thirtyfold and sixtyfold and a hundredfold." Jesse Duplantis explores this concept well in his message "Why Isn't My Giving Working? The Four Types of Giving" on YouTube.

In the Bible, we see different forms of giving: Tithes, Offerings, Alms, and Sacrificial giving. Tithing involves giving a tenth of one's income to the church, while Offerings are voluntary gifts above the tithe. Almsgiving is about helping the needy anonymously, and Sacrificial giving requires making significant personal sacrifices to help others. The story of the widow's mite in Mark 12:41-44 beautifully illustrates sacrificial giving.

Practice: Our approach to giving encompasses tithing, donating to causes, and sharing our time, skills, and resources.

The parable of the "Good Samaritan" in Luke 10:25-37 is a favorite of mine. It epitomizes the reward of giving from the heart. In this story, the Samaritan, a cultural outsider, demonstrates compassion and selflessness. His reward isn't financial; it's spiritual, a moral victory of showing love and mercy.

Laura and I have always tried to be generous, but we initially struggled with the concept of Tithing. The Bible, however, is clear about giving the first ten percent of our income. After a significant realization, we began to Tithe joyfully, without hesitation and expanded our giving to Offerings, Almsgiving, and Sacrificial contributions. This transformation in our giving was mirrored in our lives — spiritually, financially, and in our capacity to serve.

Potential: The act of giving enriches both the giver and the receiver, creating a cycle of positivity and blessings.

Throughout our 37 years of marriage, we have transitioned into giving without measure. This means giving without expecting anything in return. Our giving encompasses our time, talent, and treasure, done in obedience to God's word. The blessings we have received in return are immeasurable.

We've learned that serving and giving financially from the heart fosters a sense of stewardship and generosity. No matter our financial situation, we've found that contributing with our time and money leads to growth, both spiritually and financially. It's amazing to see how God blesses those who give selflessly.

We encourage you to reflect on your giving practices. Are you fully engaged in Tithing? Have you explored Offering, Almsgiving, and even Sacrificial giving? Stretch yourself in your giving. The satisfaction and fulfillment you will experience are beyond measure, a true testament to the joy of giving from the heart. Let's all embrace this spirit of generous giving and witness the wonderful changes it brings to our lives and those around us.

APPLIED FAITH

Taking inspiration from the heartfelt message on giving, here are three straightforward steps to integrate this spirit of generosity into your everyday life:

1. **Start Small with What You Have:** Look for simple ways to give in your daily life. This could be as easy as sharing your time to listen to a friend in need, using your skills to help someone out, or donating items you no longer use. Remember, it's not the size of the gift but the sincerity behind it that counts.

2. **Make Giving a Regular Part of Your Routine:** Set aside a little from each paycheck for Tithing or to support a cause you care about. It could also mean volunteering a few hours each month. Making this a regular habit helps cultivate a deeper sense of generosity and gratitude.

3. **Reflect on Your Giving Journey:** Take some time every now and then to think about how giving has impacted you and those around you. This reflection can be a source of joy and can motivate you to continue giving in even more meaningful ways.

DEVOTIONAL DECREE

Heavenly Father, your word states in Luke 6:38, "Give, and it will be given to you. A good measure pressed down and shaken together and running over will be poured in your lap.

For with the measure you use, it will be measured to you." I declare that Your word is true, and I stand on Your word. I declare that today, I will give my best to everyone I encounter. I am a giver. I am generous. I love to give and make a difference for others. I cast out all the lies of the enemy that would keep me from being generous in Jesus' name! My God is a God of abundance. He gave freely, so I freely gave.

7TH KEY

Stand with Gratitude

"Give thanks in all circumstances;
for this is God's will for you in Christ Jesus."
—1 Thessalonians 5:18

Purpose: Recognize the abundant blessings Jesus pours into your life and express heartfelt thanks.

Embracing gratitude has been a game-changer for us. It's like unlocking a superpower of optimism that colors the way we view life's ups and downs. Sure, it doesn't make us constantly happy – nobody's happy all the time – but it does fill us with a deep-seated appreciation for the moments and opportunities life throws our way. This shift in perspective has done wonders for our relationships and social life.

You know, being grateful has this way of making you more empathetic and understanding. It's like you're more in tune with others, and that's been a key to stronger connections in our community. And here's the cherry on top: this gratitude journey has been a health booster too! We find ourselves more motivated to take care of ourselves, whether it's sticking to a regular exercise routine, eating healthier, or just getting the right amount of sleep. It's amazing how a little gratitude can go a long way in improving your overall well-being!

Let me share with you, "I will bless the Lord at all times; his praise shall continually be in my mouth." This verse has become a guiding light in our journey to gratitude.

Let me tell you, our journey to where we are now, standing tall with gratitude, wasn't always smooth sailing. In the early days of my career, I was a bit of a hothead. Whenever a problem popped up, like a customer pointing out a defect in a product, my go-to response was defensiveness. It was never our fault, always someone else's. That mindset seeped into my team, creating this culture of finger-pointing and excuses rather than solutions. But imagine if I'd approached those moments with gratitude instead? We see each challenge as a chance to learn, improve our product, or even assist our customers better. That shift in perspective could have fostered a culture of growth and servant leadership.

This attitude spilled over into our home life, too. Laura and I weren't always cool, calm, and collected parents we strive to be today. When things went sideways, our first reaction was to raise our voices. But we learned, slowly but surely, that pausing, stepping back, and looking for the lesson in each situation was the way to go. Adopting a stance of gratitude, even in the face of chaos, opened doors to teaching and learning - not just for our kids but for us, too. Sure, there are times when you need to act fast, but responding from a place of gratitude, more often than not, steers us away from those unnecessary emotional explosions. It's about finding that grace and peace in the heat of the moment.

Maintain a gratitude journal, count your blessings daily, and offer prayers of thanksgiving.

Cultivate Gratitude: In the fast-paced world we live in, it's all too easy to get caught up in the daily grind and overlook the little moments that make life beautiful. Our culture has a penchant for focusing on divisions and setbacks, painting our days with a brush of negativity. Just take a glance at any news channel or scroll through online headlines – it's often a parade of gloom and doom. Interestingly, did you know that a social media post with an upbeat title garners only a fraction of the attention that its negatively spun counterpart does? It reveals a lot about our collective psyche and how we're attuned to respond.

But let's flip the script. We've discovered some wonderfully effective yet straightforward tools that have been game-changers in nurturing a spirit of gratitude in our lives. These practices aren't just actions; they're gateways to a more fulfilling and positive way of living. Let me share these gems with you – they're too good to keep to ourselves!

Positive affirmations: Embracing each day with positive affirmations is like opening a window to let the sunlight flood in. Each morning, as we rise, we start by giving thanks to God, setting the tone for a day filled with hope and positivity. We dive into His word, absorbing its wisdom, and then we turn our dreams into written goals, as vibrant and real as if they've already come to life. This isn't just a routine; it's a powerful ritual that infuses our whole day with a sense of deep gratitude.

But we don't stop there. To continuously remind ourselves of our purpose and identity, we've surrounded ourselves with positive affirmations and reflections of our true selves in God's eyes. These uplifting messages adorn our daily spaces - from placards in the shower to our bathroom mirrors, in our cars, and even framed on our walls. They're not just words; they're daily reminders of our journey and destination, guiding us through each day with a heart full of gratitude.

"I can do all things through him who strengthens me."
(Philippians 4:13)

"For God gave us a spirit not of fear but of power and love and self-control."
(2 Timothy 1:7)

"Love and abundance flow through me, and I attract all that I desire."

"I am grateful for all the blessings in my life, and I attract more of them each day."

GRATITUDE APPS

In our digital age, gratitude apps have become our modern-day companions in nurturing a thankful heart. They're like little beacons of positivity in the palm of our hand, offering affirmations and gentle reminders throughout the day. Laura, for instance, finds immense value in an app that sends her multiple notifications daily, each one a small prompt that realigns her focus toward gratitude. These apps aren't just tools; they're catalysts for transforming our everyday outlook.

GRATITUDE JOURNAL

Equally powerful is the timeless practice of keeping a gratitude journal. It's amazing how jotting down ten things we're thankful for each day can turn our perspective around. Our friends swear by it, saying it's like planting seeds of positivity that bloom overnight. As for us, we've found our own rhythm in ending each day with a shared prayer, giving thanks for the blessings and lessons of the day. This shared moment of reflection and gratitude strengthens our bond and aligns our hearts, reminding us of what truly matters in our lives.

IMMERSE YOURSELF IN POSITIVITY

Every day, we set aside time for activities that refresh and rejuvenate our minds. It's like a daily feast of positivity and growth. Whether it's diving into an inspiring podcast, getting lost in an enlightening video, absorbing the wisdom from the pages of a book, or sharing moments with friends who radiate positivity, these are the ingredients that flavor our day with gratitude.

POTENTIAL

A grateful heart attracts more blessings, fosters contentment, and strengthens your relationship with Jesus.

We have recently moved to a new home that we are renting. We sold all of our lawn equipment a couple of years ago and now only have a 21-inch push mower cutting an acre of grass. This seemingly mundane task has become a cherished ritual. Imagine this: twice a week, for two hours, we're immersed in enriching content, headphones on while pushing the mower through the grass. It's a five-mile walk that doubles as a personal development session. As we stride back and forth across our lawn, we're not just cutting grass; we're nurturing a garden of knowledge and gratitude in our hearts.

APPLIED FAITH

Reflecting on the value of gratitude, here are three actions you can take to develop the habit of a thankful life.

1. **Start a Daily Gratitude List:** Each day, jot down at least one thing you're thankful for. It could be as simple as a sunny day, a good meal, or a conversation that lifted your spirits. This habit helps shift your focus to the positives in your life, no matter how small.

2. **Say Thank You More:** Make it a point to express your gratitude to others. Whether it's thanking a coworker for their help or telling a friend how much you appreciate them, verbalizing your thanks can strengthen your relationships and spread positivity.

3. **End Your Day on a Positive Note:** Spend a few minutes before bed reflecting on the good parts of your day or something new you learned. This not only helps you end the day feeling more content but also sets a peaceful tone for the next day.

DEVOTIONAL DECREE

Today, I declare the goodness of God over my Life. I am grateful for the many blessings in my Life. Blessings of today and all the blessings in my future. Thank you, Lord, for your living word and your promises. Your word says in Phil 4:13, "Be anxious for nothing but in everything through prayer and supplication, with thanksgiving, make your request made known to God, and the peace of God which surpasses all understanding will guard your hearts and minds through Jesus Christ.

I am thankful for this day. I will express my gratitude to others today with my words and actions. I am thankful for my Life and everyone who is in it. I am thankful that Jesus paid the price for my sins, and I walk in that freedom daily. Thank you, thank you, thank you.

Our Walk With the 7 Keys

Over the years, Laura and I have actively practiced many of the keys we've shared with you. Often, we didn't fully realize the power of our actions or how they were shaping us into better versions of ourselves. It's only in the past five years or so that we've truly dived into studying and intentionally implementing these practices together. The transformation has been nothing short of incredible. Things we once thought impossible are now part of our reality. We've even sat down to map out our goals, something we hadn't done before, and compiled a life list of dreams and aspirations. Looking back, it's amazing to see how many of those dreams we've already brought to life.

The most transformative habit for us has been deepening our relationship with Jesus. As we focused more on this, hand in hand with unlocking our minds, our spiritual journey deepened profoundly. We've embarked on overseas mission trips, participated in local community missions, become more involved in our church, led Bible studies, and even traveled to hear messages from inspiring pastors. Our growth in faith led us to co-author "Jesus Unleashed My Potential," sharing our journey in September 2022. Our family is continually amazed at our newfound openness, patience, joy, and our relentless pursuit of positivity in every situation. Sharing how Jesus can unleash potential in all aspects of life has become our favorite conversation.

These keys have also sparked significant changes in other areas of our lives. We've taken control of our physical health with a fiery passion, diving deep into nutrition, disease prevention, exercise, and natural health methods. The transformation is tangible, **as seen in the photos below,** marking our journey from Summer 2014 to Summer 2023.

Implementing these seven keys was the catalyst for a life-altering decision in May 2021, which inspired our first book, *Jesus Unleashed My Potential.* Initially, the book was meant to detail my decision to leave a successful automotive manufacturing career to join Laura in the Juice Plus Company. However, as we surrendered our writing to God, the book evolved into something more profound - a reflection of our life's journey, the highs and lows, God's presence in it, and the lessons learned.

Since that pivotal moment in May 2021, Laura and I have been an inseparable team. Our journey has led to new friendships, interests, talents, and desires. We study, exercise, and support our family together. I've embraced new roles, from partnering with the Juice Plus Company and becoming a licensed life insurance agent to exploring alternative investments and cryptocurrency. We keep adding to our toolbox, aiming to make a meaningful difference in the lives of those we meet.

Our hope in publishing this book is to offer you a resource filled with tools, devotionals, and cherished Bible verses. We aim to inspire, empower, and equip you to navigate any situation with the reassurance that God is by your side.

God Bless.

About the J.U.M.P. Book Series

Back in May 2021, Laura and I hit a major milestone that really changed everything for us. That's when we decided to write our first book, "Jesus Unleashed My Potential." Originally, the idea was to talk about how I left a high-flying job in the car manufacturing world to join Laura over at the Juice Plus Company. It was a big shift—from being known in my field and pulling in a decent paycheck to jumping into something completely different. We thought we'd write the book together as on voice, but instead, our writing coach, David Strauss, inspired us to each write our own story and then weave them together at the end, which turned into something much bigger and better than we imagined.

It became a deep dive into our life's journey, the good times and the bad, feeling God's hand in us through it all. More than just our story, it's a helping hand for anyone else walking a similar path.

Since we made that leap, life's been full. We've made new friends, gone places, tried things we never thought we would, and really grown—both together and as individuals. It's like we're on this path of discovery, led by faith. We're closer than ever, doing everything from hitting the books to hitting the gym together. I've even branched out into new ventures like life insurance and getting into the whole cryptocurrency thing. It's all about adding more tools to our kit so we can help others more effectively.

Putting this new book out there is our way of passing on the basic ideas that have helped us move through life with faith and give you the same tools, devotionals, and bits of scripture that have been lights on our path. It'll help you find your way through the rough patches with a little more hope and a lot less worry, knowing you're not going at it alone. God has got your back, just like He's had ours.

Acknowledgements

As with our 1ˢᵗ book, we want to thank our Lord and Savior for the journey because, without Him, none of this would be possible. We are grateful for the hills and valleys that have allowed us to become who we are today.

This book has been written as an answer to prayer. Laura and I were seeking an answer from God regarding the purpose of our 1st book, "Jesus Unleashed My Potential." God did not answer us directly; rather, He chose to engage the person who helped us write and publish our first book. God provided David Strauss a vision of what was to be done. Without David reaching out to share what was provided to him in a dream, we are not sure this book would have been written, nor would any of the activities that we are working on to further the J.U.M.P. initiative.

Additionally, David made personal sacrifices to help us make this happen. He committed to spending time helping us brainstorm ideas to improve our vision, coaching us to keep us on target, being that voice of reason, and finding resources to assist with the development of our branding and book cover. That resource was none other than Barbara Wade. She was so gracious, patient, and instrumental in helping guide us through the thought process of how we wanted J.U.M.P. to be seen. Our final logo was created in collaboration with David, Barbara, and us. Thank you to both of you for committing to helping us along this journey. You both provide an example of giving without measure.

We never realized how many people it takes to write a book. Looking in reflection at each of the seven keys we have provided in this book, there are multitudes of people who either taught us, led us, or were part of the events that we learned from to be able to place us in a position to be able to share with you. The depth of knowledge and wisdom that we have been able to gain over the years has taken us drastically deeper into each area, more than we were able to portray within these pages. It is our vision to continue to build on this and to share it with you through other paths.

Understanding the key: Unlocking your mind came through many mentors. Thank you to Dr. Kenny Harless, who introduced us to understanding the power of our thoughts and of our words through the multiple lessons developed by Bob Proctor, including Thinking into Results, Lead the Field, The Science of Getting Rich, and the Success Puzzle. Also, during this training, we met so many wonderful people who we now consider to be lifelong friends, helping each other with reminders of what it takes to continually renew our minds. Thank you to Luis and Stacey Gonsalves, Dr. Jason and Misty White, Dr. Dan and Casey Grant, Kathy and Lance Muegge, and so many others. Without all of you, we would not be where we are today.

Learning to surrender our spirit, serve, and give without measure has been a lifelong journey. We feel as if things have been accelerated over the past several years, and with that reflection, there have been some key people who have contributed immensely to our spiritual growth. We want to thank our children, Anthony, Olivia, and Jason, who all continually challenge us to hold ourselves accountable for our words. Thank you to Cornerstone Church, where we felt we finally began to run. Pastors

Tim and Rhona Forsthoff planted the seed in us, providing the motivation to act with our faith.

Thanks to some of the key members of our Bible study families, including Roger and Chris Chmura, Bob and Joni Formisano, Bill and Barb Moss, Andy and Debbie Backy, Jim Kerster, and so many others who helped us grow. Thank you to Floodgate Church and Pastors Bill and Clara Bolin, who have opened our minds, hearts, and spirits to a whole new level of spiritual understanding. There are so many people who played a part, and we want to thank all of you, everyone who may not be listed here; you know who you are and that you have been a part of making an impact for us. Keep growing alongside us.

Honoring our bodies is another journey that has been a lifelong endeavor. Thank you to Joyce Buhner, who introduced us to Shaklee and provided our first real dive into nutrition. Thank you to Dr. Jason White for introducing Juice Plus to Laura. This was truly a catalyst in our drive to understand our bodies and how to ensure that they are fueled for success.

Thank you to our best trainer ever, Andre Branch, who took a chance on us. Thanks for being our training partner! Thanks to Rita Branch for allowing us to take so much of Andre's time, as well as becoming great friends. Amazing what power couples can do when they spend time together. What we learned from Andre will last our entire lives. Not only did we train together, but we also fed each other spiritually and exchanged tips for great medical care, such as functional medicine people, stem cell research, and the benefits of the sauna.

Blessing your family has always been part of our D.N.A. Thank you to Tom and Arlene Frederick and to Bob and Nancy Allmen, our parents, who modeled this and planted the seeds in us both. Thank you to Lisa and Steve Orlando, Tom and Cynthia

Frederick, Jeff Allmen, Rick Allmen, Heather Fleming, and Jim & Kelly Fleming. Our brothers, sisters, and their spouses. There are too many people to list here but know that each of you has played a key role in helping us to live out our beliefs around family each day.

We hope this book will be used by our family for generations to come. With the help and support of so many people, it is our dream to see J.U.M.P. become a movement that affects the lives of many people beyond our ability to physically reach. Only God can deliver this impact. We are merely being obedient to what He is guiding us to do.

We would like to thank Jesus,
our Lord and Savior, for the journey,
because without Him none of this
would be possible. We are grateful for
the Hills and valleys that have allowed
us to become who we are today.

www.ingramcontent.com/pod-product-compliance
Lightning Source LLC
Chambersburg PA
CBHW060351130626
46553CB00003B/1178